CONTENTS AND INSTRUCTIONS

This book belongs to

____

Can you draw a
picture of yourself?

How to use Write Size Books

Different kinds of worksheets are incorporated in this book. These different sheet types are all aimed at helping with letter formation.

These include:

Standard letter sheets in two letter sizes
- the larger to tame oversized letters and the smaller to standardize them!
Sheets grouping letters of similar shapes
Letters in alphabetical order
Pages lined to accommodate letters of the same size

- Some of the worksheets start with the letter in a dashed line format at the beginning of each row. You may notice that these dashed lines become fainter and eventually disappear, only to reappear again at the end of the line. Don't worry, this isn't a printing error!

- This unique layout is designed to maintain quality handwriting as the learner progresses along each line. As learners write, their handwriting can often deviate from the standard, legible form. The dashed guide-letters towards the end of each line are included to help bring everything back into alignment.

You have permission to create 4 duplicates of the workbook pages from this book for individual use.

THE "NO CAPITAL LETTERS" RULE

-

- Have you ever noticed children especially, mixing up capitals and lower-case letters in the same word?

    SomEtHing likE tHis.

- Learning to write lower-case letters exclusively can prevent this. When lower-case letter writing has been mastered, we can learn capitals.

- After all, we don't use capital letters very often, so why present them at the same time and just confuse the learner?

- After learning capital letters, then we can stick them at the beginning of sentences and on proper nouns.

    Of course... that comes later.

PRACTICE SCHEDULE

- ## WEEK 1: Letters a, b, c

1. **DAY 1** – Letter a (Bigger letters)

2. **DAY 2** – Letter a (Smaller letters)

3. **DAY 3** – Letter b (Bigger letters)

4. **DAY 4** – Letter b (Smaller letters)

5. **DAY 5** – Letter c (Bigger letters)

6. **DAY 6** – Letter c (Smaller letters)

7. **DAY 7** – Bigger and smaller letters a, b, and c. Try free writing on lined paper to see if this has affected the writing size and uniformity. If not, then repeat the same process

You have permission to create 4 duplicates of the workbook pages from this book for individual use. For additional content, consider our expanded edition with numerous extra pages. Available on our website.

- ## WEEK 2: Letters d, e, f

8. **DAY 8** – Letter d (Bigger letters)

9. **DAY 9** – Letter d (Smaller letters)

10. **DAY 10** – Letter e (Bigger letters)

11. **DAY 11** – Letter e (Smaller letters)

12. **DAY 12** – Letter f (Bigger letters)

13. **DAY 13** – Letter f (Smaller letters)

14. **DAY 14** – Bigger and smaller letters a, b, c, d, e, and f. Try free writing on lined paper to see if this has affected handwriting size and uniformity. If not, then repeat the same process.

- ## WEEK 3: Letters g, h, i as before

21. On **DAY 21** – Bigger and smaller letters a, b, c, d, e, f, g, h, and i. Try free writing on lined paper

Continue the process until all the letters have been covered.

Similar letters are covered at the end to ensure that the learner can distinguish between them. Additionally, prompt the learner to pronounce the letters aloud, ensuring recognition!

Accelerated Schedule for Ages 6 and Up:

- For learners aged six and above, consider covering two letters per day (a and b big then the next day a and b small) while following a similar sequence.

Note:

- It is essential to adapt the schedule according to the learners' needs and abilities, including repeating phases.

- As learners' capacity can vary widely, feel free to explore different variations to find the most effective learning pace.

The small letter alphabet

▼ This symbol indicates the starting point and the direction to follow

Remind the learner to do two things while writing...

To repeat the mantra guiding letter formation (round → up etc.)

To take their time and not rush!

 Mantra audio recordings are available on our website

www.write.education

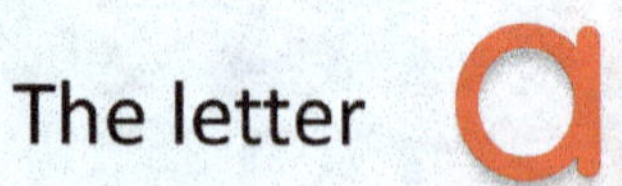

The letter a

Keep going... Go slowly

Remember to keep below the line

The letter a

Keep going... Go slowly

Remember to keep below the line

© 2023 WRITE EDUCATION

The letter 

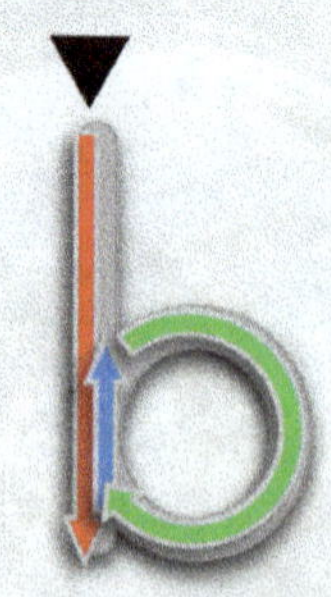

Keep going... Go slowly

WRITE EDUCATION

The letter 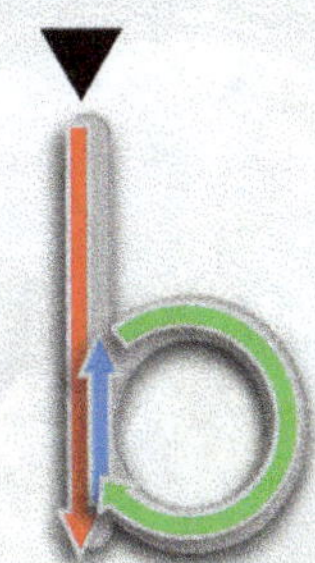

Keep going... Go slowly

The letter 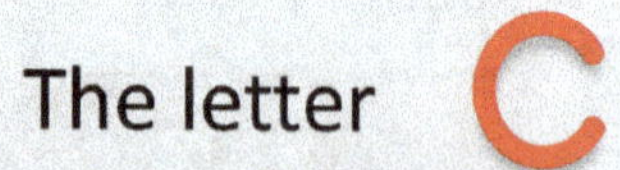

Round

STOP!

Don't make a circle

Keep going... Go slowly

Remember to keep below the line

The letter 

Keep going... Go slowly

Remember to keep below the line

© 2023 WRITE EDUCATION

The letter 

Keep going... Go slowly

Keep going... Go slowly

The letter 

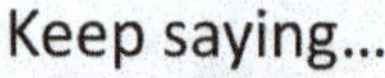

STOP! 

Keep going... Go slowly

Remember to keep below the line

© 2023 WRITE EDUCATION

The letter 

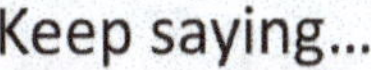

Keep going... Go slowly

Remember to keep below the line

© 2023 WRITE EDUCATION

The letter 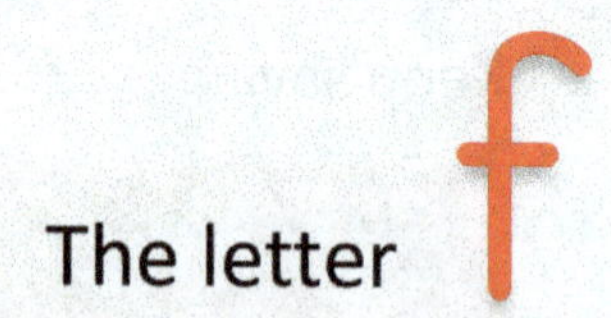

Keep going... Go slowly

The letter 

Keep going... Go slowly

The letter g

Keep going... Go slowly

Remember to keep below the line

The letter 

Keep going... Go slowly

Remember to keep below the line

Well done!

The letter 

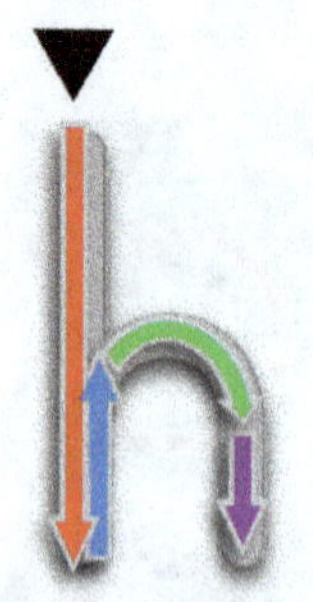

Keep going... Go slowly

The letter 

Keep going… Go slowly

WRITE SIZE

The letter i

Keep going... Go slowly

Remember to keep below the line

The letter 

Keep going... Go slowly

Remember to keep below the line

WRITE SIZE

The letter j

Keep going... Go slowly

Remember to keep below the line

The letter j

Keep going... Go slowly

Remember to keep below the line

© 2023 WRITE EDUCATION

The letter k 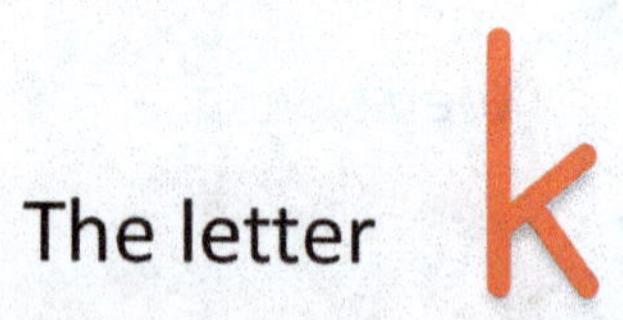

Keep saying...

Keep going... Go slowly

The letter 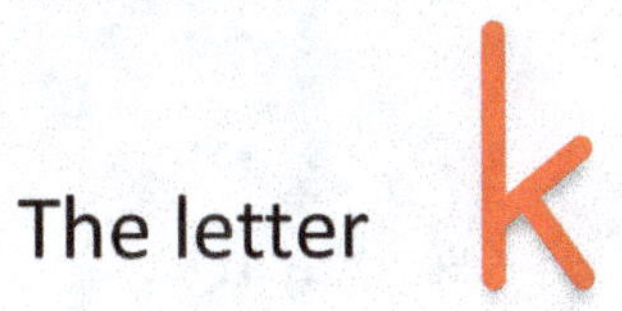

Keep saying...

Keep going... Go slowly

© 2023 WRITE EDUCATION

The letter |

Keep saying...

Down Down

STOP!

Keep going... Go slowly

The letter |

Keep saying...

Down Down

STOP!

Keep going... Go slowly

WRITE SIZE

The letter 

Keep going... Go slowly

Remember to keep below the line

The letter 

Keep going... Go slowly

Remember to keep below the line

Well done!

© 2023 WRITE EDUCATION

The letter 

Keep going... Go slowly

Remember to keep below the line

The letter 

Keep saying...

Keep going... Go slowly

Remember to keep below the line

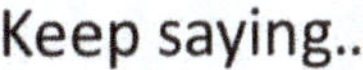

The letter 

 or 

Keep saying...

Round

Remember to keep below the line

The letter 

 or 

Keep saying...

Round

Keep going... Go slowly

Remember to keep below the line

Well done!

© 2023 WRITE EDUCATION

The letter 

Keep going... Go slowly

Remember to keep below the line

The letter 

Keep going... Go slowly

Remember to keep below the line

The letter 

Round

Up

Down Down

Keep going... Go slowly

Remember to keep below the line

The letter q

Keep going... Go slowly

Remember to keep below the line

© 2023 WRITE EDUCATION

The letter **r**

Keep going... Go slowly

Remember to keep below the line

The letter r

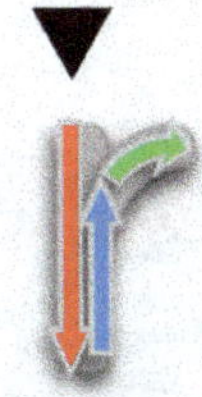

Keep going... Go slowly

Remember to keep below the line

The letter 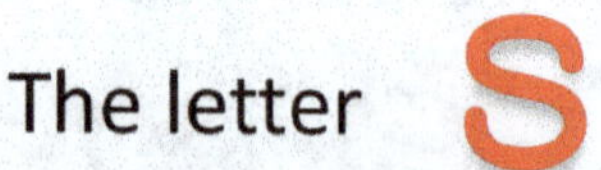

Keep going… Go slowly

Remember to keep below the line

Keep going... Go slowly

Remember to keep below the line

WRITE SIZE

The letter 

Keep going... Go slowly

The letter 

Keep saying...

Keep going... Go slowly

© 2023 WRITE EDUCATION

The letter 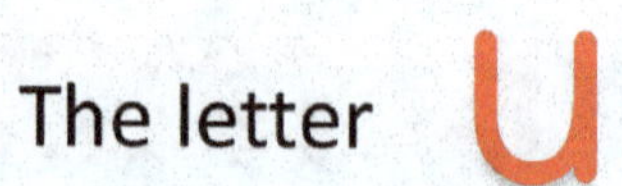

Keep going... Go slowly

Remember to keep below the line

The letter 

Keep going... Go slowly

Remember to keep below the line

© 2023 WRITE EDUCATION

The letter 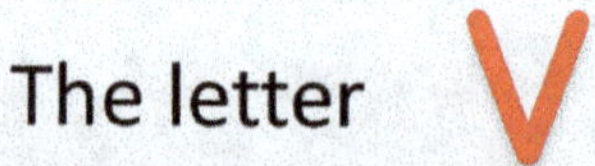

Down Diagonal

Up Diagonal

Keep going... Go slowly

Remember to keep below the line

The letter V

Keep going... Go slowly

Remember to keep below the line

Well done!

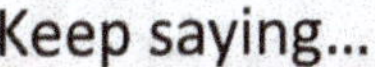

The letter W

Keep saying...

Down Diagonal	(orange)
Up Diagonal	(blue)
Down Diagonal	(green)
Up Diagonal	(purple)

Keep going... Go slowly

Remember to keep below the line

© 2023 WRITE EDUCATION

The letter 

Keep going... Go slowly

Remember to keep below the line

© 2023 WRITE EDUCATION

The letter 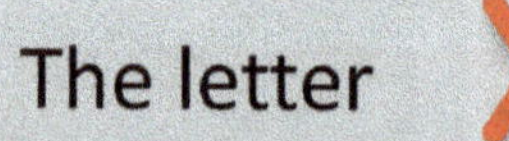

Keep going... Go slowly

Remember to keep below the line

Keep going... Go slowly

Remember to keep below the line

© 2023 WRITE EDUCATION

The letter 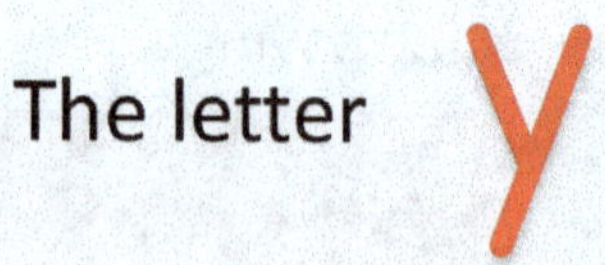

Keep going... Go slowly

Remember to keep below the line

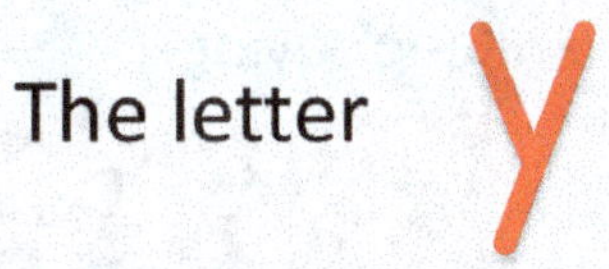

The letter **y**

Keep going... Go slowly

Remember to keep below the line

Well done!

© 2023 WRITE EDUCATION.

The letter z

Keep saying...
Line to the Right
Down Diagonal
Line to the Right

Keep going... Go slowly

Remember to keep below the line

The letter 

Keep going... Go slowly

Remember to keep below the line

Similar Letters

Keep going... Go slowly

Keep going... Go slowly

Similar Letters

Keep going… Go slowly

Similar Letters

Keep going... Go slowly

Keep going... Go slowly

Similar Letters

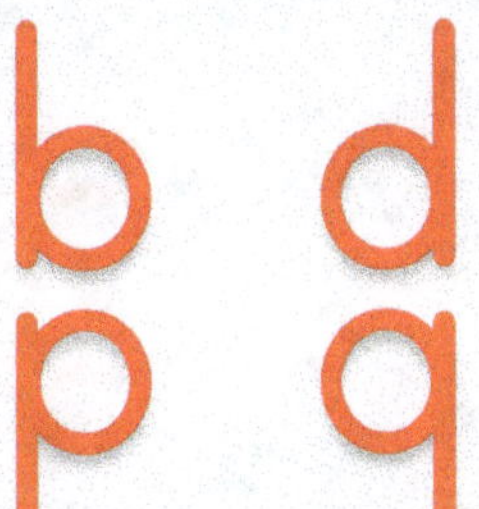

Keep going... Go slowly

Similar Letters

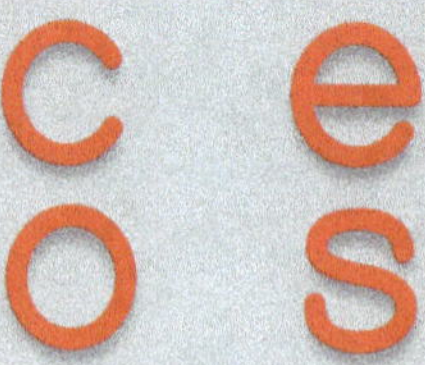

Keep going... Go slowly

Similar Letters

Keep going... Go slowly

Similar Letters

h m n r u

Keep going... Go slowly

h m n r u

Keep going... Go slowly

The Alphabet

a to k

The Alphabet

Keep going... Go slowly

a a a a
b b b b
c c c c
d d d d
e e e e
f f f f
g g g g
h h h h
i i i i
j j j j
k k k k

l to u

Keep going... Go slowly

l l l l			
m m m m			
n n n n			
o o o o			
p p p p			
q q q q			
r r r r			
s s s s			
t t t t			
u u u u			

The Alphabet

l to u

Keep going... Go slowly

© 2023 WRITE EDUCATION

The Alphabet

v to z

Keep going... Go slowly

v v v v

w w w

x x x x

y y y y

z z z z

The Alphabet

v to z

Keep going... Go slowly

Congratulations!
You have reached the end of this book.

You have done so well!
All of us on our team are very proud of you!

Thank you for purchasing this book.
We hope that it helped for handwriting practice.

- Visit our website at www.write.education for more.

- Many new products are in development.

  At our website, you can sign up to stay updated on new products and subscribe to our insightful newsletter focusing on early-years education.

- On our website you can also purchase
  - Via Amazon, our expanded edition with numerous extra pages
  - Audio recordings of the letter formation mantras

  Any questions or suggestions, feel free to email us at getintouch@write.education

Send an email

Visit the website